Biography.

Winston CHURCHILL

Janice Hamilton

Twenty-First Century Books
Minneapolis

This book is dedicated to the three wonderful men in my life: my husband, Harold, and my sons, Michael and David.

Twenty-First Century Books
A division of Lerner Publishing Group
241 First Avenue North
Minneapolis, MN 55401 U.S.A.

Website addresses: www.lernerbooks.com
www.biography.com

Library of Congress Cataloging-in-Publication Data

Hamilton, Janice.
    Winston Churchill / by Janice Hamilton.
       p. cm. — (A&E biography)
    Includes bibliographical references and index.
    ISBN–13: 978–0–8225–3419–8 (lib. bdg. : alk. paper)
    ISBN–10: 0–8225–3419–3 (lib. bdg. : alk. paper)
    1. Churchill, Winston, Sir, 1874–1965. 2. Great Britain—Politics and government—20th century. 3. Prime ministers—Great Britain—Biography. I. Title. II. Series: A&E biography (Twenty-First Century Books (Firm))
    DA566.9.C5H245 2006
    941.084'092—dc22 [B]   2005017294

Manufactured in the United States of America
1 2 3 4 5 6 – BP – 11 10 09 08 07 06

CONTENTS

British prime minister Winston Churchill makes the V-for-victory sign during World War II (1939–1945). This hand gesture came to be closely associated with Churchill.

PROLOGUE: A WARTIME LEADER

In 1940 British prime minister Winston Spencer Churchill led a nation at war. For the previous eleven years, he had been out of government office. He had warned in vain that Adolf Hitler's Nazi Germany was a threat to European peace and democracy. Few people had taken him seriously, and Great Britain, an island nation, lacked the airplanes and military equipment necessary even to defend itself. But in September 1939, when Nazi troops invaded Poland, a country that Britain had promised to defend, Britain found itself at war.

Government leaders invited Churchill to join the war cabinet that would direct Britain's war strategy. On May 10, 1940, he became prime minister. Three days later, he made one of the most famous speeches in British parliamentary history. He told the House of Commons, "I have nothing to offer but blood, toil, tears, and sweat. . . .

"You ask, what is our policy? I will say: It is to wage war, by sea, land, and air, with all our might and with all the strength that God can give us: to wage war against a monstrous tyranny, never surpassed in the dark, lamentable catalogue of human crime. That is our policy."

Newly appointed prime minister Winston Churchill, center, *leaves his home in London on May 10, 1940. Three days later, he would give his famous "Blood, Toil, Tears, and Sweat," speech to the British Parliament.*

"You ask, What is our aim? I can answer in one word: victory, victory, at all costs, victory, in spite of all terror, victory, however long and hard the road may be; for without victory, there is no survival."

It was as if Churchill had been preparing for this moment all his life. History had presented a situation where he could—he must—succeed. He was sixty-five years old, an age at which many politicians retired from public life. He had already experienced adventures around the world, become a successful and well-paid writer, raised a family, and held some of the highest political offices in the land. But for Churchill, these dark days turned out to be his finest hour.

N°. 28,176.

BIRTHS.

On the 30th Nov., at Blenheim Palace, the Lady RANDOLPH CHURCHILL, prematurely, of a son.

On the 7th Oct., at Rangoon, the wife of HALKETT F. JACKSON, Esq., Lieut. and Adjutant 67th Regt., of a daughter.

On the 20th Oct., at Bombay, the wife of Capt. G. W. OLDHAM, R.E., of a son.

On the 27th Oct., at Ranchi, Chota Nagpore, the wife of Capt. NINIAN LOWIS, B.S.C., Assistant Commissioner, of a daughter.

On the 6th Nov., 1874, at Belgaum, India, the wife of J. CHARLES M. PIGOTT, Esq., Lieut. 66th Regt., of a daughter.

On the 20th Nov., at Marlborough-terrace, Roath, Cardiff, the wife of THOMAS J. ALLEN, of a daughter.

On the 21st Nov., the wife of POYNTZ WRIGHT, M.R.C.S.E., of a daughter.

On the 22d Nov., at South-hill-park, Hampstead, the wife of ALBERT STRAUBE, of a son.

On the 26th Nov., at Wolfang, Queensland, Australia, the wife of HENRY DE SATGÊ, Esq., of a son.

On the 27th Nov., at Wolverton House, Bucks, the wife of SPENCER R. HARRISON, Esq., of a daughter.

On the 28th Nov., at Eton College, the wife of ARTHUR C. JAMES, Esq., of a daughter.

On the 28th Nov., at Churt Vicarage, near Farnham, the wife of the Rev. A. B. ALEXANDER, of a daughter.

On the 29th Nov., at 31, Spencer-square, Ramsgate, the wife of Mr. GEO. HAWKINS, late of Brighton, of a son.

On the 29th Nov., at Kibworth Beauchamp, Leicestershire, the wife of THOMAS MACAULAY, Surgeon, of a daughter.

On the 29th Nov., at Nunthorpe Grove, York, Mrs. WOOD CLARKE, of a son.

On the 29th Nov., at Oakbraes, Godalming, the wife of Major A. OLIVER RUTHERFURD, of a son.

On the 29th Nov., at 30, rue Royale, Tours, the wife of Monsieur ALFRED HAINGUERLOT, of a son.

On the 30th Nov., at 10, Talbot-road, Westbourne-park, W., the wife of V. C. DE RIVAZ, of a daughter.

On the 30th Nov., at Bayfield, Southsea, the wife of L. HOLLAND REIDE, of a son.

This column from the Times (London) announces the birth of Winston Churchill, first entry, in 1874.

Chapter **ONE**

A LONELY
CHILDHOOD

WINSTON LEONARD SPENCER CHURCHILL WAS BORN on November 30, 1874, at Blenheim Palace, in Oxfordshire, England. His mother was staying at the palace (the home of her parents-in-law, the Duke and Duchess of Marlborough) when she went into labor. The doctor she had expected would attend the birth in London could not come, but the local doctor delivered the baby safely.

Winston was born into one of the most famous families in Great Britain. He was a descendant of John Churchill, first Duke of Marlborough (1650–1722). That duke was a great army general who led Queen Anne's British troops and their allies to a series of victories over Louis XIV of France in the early 1700s. In gratitude, Parliament had Blenheim Palace built as a gift for the duke. It became one of the country's finest architectural treasures.

After the first duke died, the title and the palace were passed down to succeeding generations of family members. Most of them were described as extravagant, unstable, bad-tempered, and depressed individuals. Winston's grandfather, however, the seventh Duke of Marlborough, was known to be a man of strong moral and religious beliefs.

Lord Randolph Churchill (Winston's father) was his third son. Under English custom, only the eldest son inherits the title and the palace, so Lord Randolph had to find a career. He chose politics. He was first elected to the House of Commons a year before Winston was born. Because members of Parliament were unpaid at that time, Lord Randolph was always short of money, and his father had to help him financially.

Winston's mother was Jennie Jerome, the beautiful, Brooklyn-born daughter of Leonard Jerome, a stockbroker, a former part-owner of the *New York Times*, and a horse racing fan. In 1867, when Jennie was thirteen, her mother took her and her sisters to Europe for a few years to further their education and expand their social lives. Jennie met Lord Randolph in August 1873, at a ball on the Isle of Wight, off the southern coast of England. The two were immediately attracted to each other, and within three days, they were engaged. They were married in a small ceremony

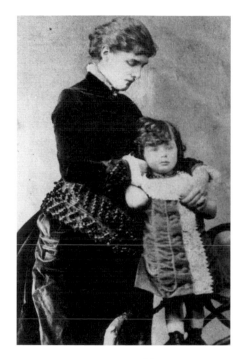

Lady Randolph Churchill holds her son Winston in the 1870s. Most of the time, a nanny cared for Winston during his early childhood.

at the British Embassy in Paris on April 15, 1874. Winston was born seven and a half months later.

As was the custom, Lady Randolph hired a nanny to look after Winston. Her name was Anne Everest, but Winston called her Woom, baby talk for *woman*. His closest companion, she cared for his every need. Still, Winston adored his mother. "She shone for me like the Evening Star. I loved her dearly—but at a distance," he said. She was too busy leading a glamorous life to spend much time with him, although she did sometimes take him for walks or read him stories.

In 1877 Lord Randolph's work took the family to Ireland, then part of the United Kingdom of Great Britain and Ireland. Churchill later recalled his earliest childhood memory was of watching his grandfather the duke unveil a statue in Dublin. In Ireland his parents hired a governess (private tutor) for Winston. The youngster was a reluctant student. The first day she came to the house, he hid in the bushes for hours. After that, he found reading was easy, but arithmetic mystified him. "The figures were tied into all sorts of tangles and did things to one another which it was extremely difficult to forecast with complete accuracy," he complained.

Winston's brother John (better known as Jack) was born in 1880. Later that year, the family returned to London.

BOARDING SCHOOL

When Winston was just seven, he was sent away to a boarding school, where he lived full-time. He hated it. Although he did well in subjects he enjoyed, like history and geography, the required subject of Latin made about as much sense to him as math did. Furthermore, his teachers considered his behavior extremely difficult, and they sometimes beat him—a common punishment at many British schools. He finally got revenge—and a reputation for defiance that lasted long after he left the school—by kicking the headmaster's (principal's) favorite straw hat to pieces.

Winston's health was poor, and his parents decided to send him to school in coastal Brighton. The family doctor, who practiced there as well as in London, promised to keep an eye on him. The teachers were kind, and although he had few close friends, he enjoyed acting in the school plays and did well in his class work. On the whole, he was happy there.

Winston wrote to his parents regularly. He often asked his mother to send money—he was usually

When Winston was seven years old, left, *his parents sent him away to a boarding school, which he hated.*

short of funds. He also asked her to visit and was disappointed when she did not come. On two occasions, Winston found out that his father had been in Brighton on business, and he was upset that Lord Randolph had not come to see him. Often his parents were traveling abroad when he was on holiday, so he spent many vacations with Woom and his brother or at Blenheim Palace.

In 1886, when Winston was eleven, he came down with pneumonia at school. For several days, he had a very high fever, and the doctor was worried that he might not survive. His parents arrived, and the doctor stayed by his bedside until the danger was over. It took him several months to regain his strength.

Two years later, Winston began to prepare for his entrance examinations for Harrow, an elite boarding school. He studied hard and looked forward to going there, but nervous excitement got the better of him. Not only did the examiners test him on the hated Latin, rather than the history he loved, but "they always tried to ask what I did not know," he recalled. "When I would have willingly displayed my knowledge, they sought to expose my ignorance. This sort of treatment had only one result: I did not do well in examinations."

This meant that Winston was placed in the class with the slower boys. He soon realized this brought a big advantage. Rather than having to study Greek and Latin, his class concentrated on English. "Thus I got into my bones the essential structure of the ordinary British sentence—which is a noble thing."

The assistant headmaster complained to his mother about his "carelessness, unpunctuality [lateness] and irregularity in every way." His main achievement at Harrow was the school prize he received for reciting perfectly by heart twelve hundred lines of poetry. In his final year, he won a fencing championship.

Winston stands in a fine suit at about the time of his studies at Harrow School. While at the school, the twelve-year-old was put in classes with slower learners and mastered English.

During school breaks, Winston spent hours with his collection of fifteen hundred miniature lead soldiers, lining them up in battle formation to replay his famous ancestor's victories. His father, seeing this interest in the military, decided that Winston should have a career in the army. Actually, Lord Randolph was convinced that Winston was too stupid to go to university or law school, but Winston did not know this and was happy with the choice.

The next hurdle was to prepare for the entrance exams to the Royal Military Academy at Sandhurst, the training school for future officers. After failing twice, Winston studied with a tutor who specialized in helping boys cram for the army entrance exams.

SANDHURST

As he entered Sandhurst in September 1893, his father had a stern warning for him. Lord Randolph wrote, "I am certain that if you cannot prevent yourself from leading the idle useless unprofitable life you have had during your schooldays and later months, you will . . . degenerate into a shabby unhappy and futile existence." His old nanny, Anne Everest, had gentler advice: "Don't expose yourself to the sun this hot weather, dear," and "Don't run into debt or keep bad company."

Winston made many friends at Sandhurst. He loved riding horses and did well in topics such as fortification, tactics, mapmaking, military law, and military

Rise and Fall

Lord Randolph Churchill was a bright star in politics, but he quickly self-destructed. In 1886 he was appointed chancellor of the exchequer, in charge of finances. This was the second-highest position in the country, after the prime minister. He was only thirty-seven years old, and some people were jealous of his rapid rise to power.

Lord Randolph was very intelligent and an excellent public speaker, but he often quarreled with his colleagues and acted without thinking. When he proposed a budget that included funding cuts for the navy and war offices, the ministers responsible for these services protested. In response, Lord Randolph offered to resign. He intended the offer as a warning that he was serious, but the prime minister, who did not like him, accepted his resignation, and his political career crashed. Winston's faith in his father remained steadfast, however.

administration. He graduated fifteen months later, eighth in a class of 150.

Meanwhile, Lord Randolph's health had been declining for several years, although he remained a member of Parliament. Family members believed he was suffering from the long-term effects of syphilis, a sexually transmitted disease that, when untreated, eventually affects the brain. Some medical experts suspect he actually had a brain tumor. Whatever the cause, his speech was slurred, his thoughts muddled, and he was often extremely angry, especially with his older son. Lord Randolph died on January 24, 1895, a few weeks before his fifty-sixth birthday. "All my dreams of comradeship with him, of entering Parliament at his side and in his support, were ended," Winston wrote later. "There remained for me only to pursue his aims and vindicate his memory."

Winston's father, Lord Randolph Churchill, left, *showed very little confidence in his son. Lord Randolph died in 1895.*

Winston's relationship with his father was one of the most difficult and important of his life. He deeply admired Lord Randolph and craved his attention and approval. He seldom received either. But even long after his father's death, Winston needed to prove that he was not the failure his father saw in him.

At the age of twenty-one, Churchill, above, *became a British military officer and commanded a cavalry unit.*

Chapter **TWO**

OFFICER, JOURNALIST, AND POLITICIAN

CHURCHILL WAS NOW TWENTY-ONE YEARS OLD AND launched on a military career. He had red hair, pink skin, and a round face. He was just over five feet six inches tall and walked with a slight stoop. Although his health was never strong, he soon proved he had plenty of courage.

He became an officer in the Fourth Hussars, a cavalry (mounted on horseback) regiment, where he was in charge of about thirty men. It was an expensive life, as an officer had to pay for uniforms and for upkeep of his horses. His father had left the family little money, but his Blenheim relatives helped out. And his mother, still beautiful in her forties, was reputed to have many lovers and knew many men in important positions.

Churchill had vacation time coming. He decided to go to Cuba, where local rebels were fighting against a corrupt Spanish colonial government. His mother spoke with the British ambassador to Spain, and Churchill received permission to join Spanish troops fighting the rebels. He also arranged to collect technical information for British military intelligence and to write some articles for a London newspaper. After spending a short time with Jerome relatives in New York City, Churchill and a friend arrived in Cuba in November 1895.

Rebel bullets whizzed close to him on several occasions as he rode through the Cuban countryside with the Spanish soldiers, and he found these encounters with danger exhilarating. Even so, he sympathized with the Cuban people's desire for independence. He noted the success of their hit-and-run guerrilla tactics as they burned agricultural fields, shot at camps of sleeping soldiers, and blew up trains.

In September 1896, Churchill's British regiment sailed for India (part of the British Empire at that time), and once there, he settled into a leisurely life in the mountain city of Bangalore. He and two fellow officers shared a spacious bungalow and several servants. He grew roses, collected butterflies, and played polo. He also continued his education. Lady Randolph sent him a huge pile of books on history, economics, and philosophy, as well as parliamentary debates. Thus Churchill gave himself the education he felt he would need to

Churchill on his mount while stationed in India in 1896. He did not see military combat, but he studied hard and played polo.

pursue his long-term goal, a career in politics. What he missed, however, was sharing ideas with other students at a university, and he never did learn to listen to other people's opinions.

The following year, while on holiday in England, Churchill heard that the British were planning a military expedition to punish rebel tribesmen near the northwest border of India, near Afghanistan.

The expedition leader had once promised Churchill he could go along on his next mission. Churchill rushed back to India, obtained permission to take an extended leave from his regiment, and followed the expedition as a journalist. The result was his first book, *The Story of the Malakand Field Force.* It received a great deal of attention, and even the Prince of Wales (later King Edward VII) admired it.

Churchill was determined to achieve fame, and he decided the best way to do so was to put himself in the midst of military action and then write about it. He wanted to go to Sudan. The British were sending a military expedition to help Egypt, which they controlled, conquer Sudan—located south of Egypt on the upper reaches of the Nile River. But General Sir Herbert Kitchener, who was in charge of the force, considered Churchill a medal hunter. He refused him permission to join the troops.

Churchill was never shy about going to the top when he wanted something. He asked for the help of the British prime minister, who had admired his book. He received permission to join the expedition, and he reached Cairo, Egypt, in August 1898. From there he traveled up the Nile to Sudan, where he took part in the last-ever British cavalry charge at the bloody Battle of Omdurman. Thousands of enemy soldiers died, and Churchill believed he personally killed several.

He returned to India for a few months. There, he started researching and writing *The River War,* his book about Sudan, and he took part in a big polo tournament. He also considered his future and decided to resign from the military and concentrate on writing and politics.

PRISON AND ESCAPE

Back in Britain, Churchill ran for a seat in Parliament for the first time in 1899, but he was defeated. Soon after, another opportunity for adventure arose. Great Britain was about to go to war in southern Africa with the Boers (the region's Dutch settlers) to gain control of the Dutch colony and its recently discovered diamond and gold mines. Churchill arranged to cover the war for London's *Morning Post* newspaper and set sail for Durban, a port in the British colony of Natal, on the east coast of southern Africa.

From Durban he boarded an armored train to the embattled interior town of Ladysmith. When the Boers ambushed the train and several cars were derailed, Churchill showed great bravery and leadership. He helped the wounded, persuaded the terrified civilian train engineer to stay at the controls, and helped him remove some of the derailed cars from the track. Remaining at the derailment site when the train retreated, Churchill suddenly found himself confronted by an armed Boer soldier on horseback. He recalled, "I thought there was absolutely no chance of escape; if he fired he would surely hit me, so I held up my hands and surrendered myself a prisoner of war."

Churchill, a military journalist, exits his tent in Bloemfontein, South Africa, shortly after his capture and escape during the Boer War (1899–1902).

The Boers took Churchill to a prison camp in the town of Pretoria. He and several other officers planned to escape together, but only Churchill actually got over the fence. He spoke no Afrikaans (the Boer language), and the Boers were very anxious to recapture their escapee. But luck was with him. He chanced to knock on the door of the only Englishman for miles around. This man, who worked as a mine manager, hid him for several days in a mine shaft and then smuggled him on board a freight train bound for a neighboring Portuguese colony. By the time

Churchill arrived back in Durban, just before Christmas 1899, the story of his escape had spread throughout the British Empire.

Churchill stayed in southern Africa for another six months, working as a journalist and also serving as an officer. He narrowly escaped injury several times and observed the horror of death on the battlefield close up. He also developed a strong admiration for the Boer fighters. After returning to England, he wrote two books about the Boer War and went on a well-paying lecture tour to speak about it to audiences in Britain, Canada, and the United States.

SAVED AGAIN

Churchill often worried that, like his father, he would die young. He was often ill as a child, and he was accident-prone. In 1893, when he was nineteen, he fell twenty-nine feet from a tree during a game and had to spend several months recovering in bed. Later that year, he and Jack nearly drowned while swimming in a lake in Switzerland. During his military career, Churchill was often in danger and often narrowly escaped injury. After repeatedly surviving these brushes with death, he concluded that fate was saving him for some greater purpose.

Back home, Churchill ran in the general election of 1900, and this time he won a seat by a narrow margin. He was finally a member of Parliament—at the age of twenty-six. Only four days after taking his seat in the House of Commons, he made his first speech there. In preparation for public life, he practiced over and over the sentence "The Spanish ships I cannot see, for they are not in sight" in hopes of making his lisp—he pronounced the letter *s* like *sh*—less noticeable.

Churchill was a member of the Conservative Party, his father's party, and the political home of most of Britain's wealthy and aristocratic elite. But he disagreed with the Conservatives on many important

Churchill in 1900. In a close race, Churchill won his first election to Parliament that year.

issues. He was shocked when he read a book that described the extreme poverty and terrible housing conditions found in the town of York, and he felt the government should do more to help the poor. "I see little glory in an Empire which can rule the waves and is unable to flush its sewers," he wrote in a letter to a leading Conservative.

SWITCHING SIDES

In 1904 he joined the opposition Liberal Party. In abandoning the Conservatives, however, he lost some old friends and angered several of his relatives and colleagues.

In spite of this, in the general election of 1906, Churchill was elected in a Liberal landslide. It was an important year for Churchill in other ways too. His biography of his father was published, and he was appointed a junior-level minister, undersecretary of state at the colonial office. At that time, the British Empire covered the globe, with colonies from India and Africa to the Caribbean. Churchill was intensely proud of the empire.

That summer he met Violet Asquith, daughter of the prime minister. They became lifelong friends. She later recalled that he launched into a one-sided discussion of the shortness of human life and the immense possibility of human accomplishment, ending with the pronouncement, "We are all worms. But I do believe that I am a glow-worm."

Churchill loved the fun of politics and enjoyed the way unexpected events kept things from becoming too predictable. His opponents often called him irrational, and he cheerfully agreed they were right. He believed in democracy, but not in opinion polls. He said, "It is not a good thing always to be feeling your pulse and taking your temperature. Although one has to do it sometimes, you do not want to make a habit of it. I have heard it said that a Government should keep its ear to the ground, but they would also remember that this is not a very dignified attitude."

A Social Reformer

In 1908, at the age of thirty-three, Churchill became one of the youngest senior cabinet ministers in British history. As president of the board of trade, he introduced revolutionary new approaches to help Britain's poor and working-class people, including unemployment insurance and a network of labor exchanges to help unemployed laborers find work. These and other measures helped lay the foundations for what later became Britain's extensive social welfare program.

Churchill was never terribly interested in women—politics kept him too busy—although he had been in love several times. When he first met Clementine Hozier a few years earlier, he paid little attention to her. But when he sat next to her at a dinner party in April 1908, he found the twenty-two-year-old Clementine to be very intelligent, and her strong character

Churchill proposed to Clementine Hozier, left, at Blenheim Palace in August 1908. The couple were married in the fall of that year.

appealed to him. In early August, he took her to Blenheim Palace, where he proposed in the garden. They were married in September. Even with such short notice, thirteen hundred guests attended the wedding. The couple's first child, Diana, was born in 1909.

In 1910 Churchill became home secretary, with police and prisons among his responsibilities. He sympathized with prisoners, having been one himself, and he introduced a number of reforms to the prison system. On the other hand, when a series of violent labor strikes broke out, he took a hard line. Many of the strikers and their union leaders wanted to overhaul British society. While Churchill was in favor of social reforms, he was essentially a conservative person and was not willing to listen to demands for radical change.

In November 1910, striking miners rioted and damaged property in the village of Tonypandy, Wales. Churchill ordered extra police from London to reinforce local police forces and organized a meeting between strike leaders and mediators, officials working to find a solution agreeable to both sides. Meanwhile, military troops waited nearby in case the police

Police stand ready to take on striking coal miners in Tonypandy, Wales. When Churchill called in the police and the military to control the strikers, he was praised and criticized for his actions. Eventually negotiations brought the strike to a peaceful conclusion.

needed extra help. When the strike was over, some people praised Churchill for the way in which he had handled the situation. But labor leaders criticized him for being too aggressive, and Conservatives said he had not been tough enough.

In May 1911, Clementine gave birth to the couple's only son, Randolph. In June the Churchills rode in a procession through the streets of London during the coronation of King George V and Queen Mary.

A few weeks later, there was further labor unrest. Dock and railway workers went on strike across the country, disrupting the distribution of food. There were riots and violent confrontations between police and strikers. During one such incident, military troops arrived. When the demonstrators threw rocks at the soldiers, the soldiers fired, killing two civilians. Although Churchill sympathized with the badly paid dockworkers and peace was restored by the end of summer, these events tarnished his reputation with working- class people.

Churchill was in his mid-thirties, he had begun a family, and his political career seemed well on track. But it was about to change directions again.

First Lord of the Admiralty Winston Churchill, left, *walks with Admiral Lord Fischer in 1911.*

Chapter **THREE**

THE GREAT WAR

CHURCHILL FORGOT ALL ABOUT SOCIAL REFORM WHEN he was appointed first lord of the admiralty, in charge of Britain's navy, in October 1911. Great Britain, an island nation and head of a vast empire, required a strong navy. Churchill threw himself into the job. He visited naval facilities, learned about naval guns and tactics, enlarged and modernized the fleet, improved morale, and kept an eye on Germany as it rapidly enlarged its navy.

Airplanes also fascinated Churchill. He discussed the potential role that naval airplanes could play in war and invented the word *seaplane*. In 1913 he began flying lessons. In the early days, flying was a dangerous pastime, but Churchill found it thrilling. Neither

Churchill and Clementine stand beside an airplane in the early 1900s. Churchill had a fascination with the new world of aviation.

Clementine nor his friends approved, and he gave it up after his instructor was killed in a crash.

As first lord, Churchill had an office and living quarters on board the admiralty yacht *Enchantress*, with its crew of 196, so he spent a lot of time away from the family. Later, Clementine and the children were able to move with him into Admiralty House, the grand official residence in London.

Meanwhile, a combination of factors, including economic rivalries, an arms race, and growing nationalism, were increasing tensions in Europe. By 1914 war seemed imminent. At the end of July, a united Austria-

Hungary declared war on Serbia, and Britain prepared for possible involvement in the conflict.

Churchill wrote his wife from the admiralty, "My darling one and beautiful, Everything tends towards catastrophe and collapse. I am interested, geared up and happy. Is it not horrible to be built like that? The preparations have a hideous fascination for me. I pray to God to forgive me for such fearful moods of levity. Yet I would do my best for peace, & nothing would induce me to wrongfully strike the blow."

Many Britons did not want to get involved in a war. But Britain was allied by treaty with France and Russia and had an agreement to help neutral Belgium if it was invaded. After Germany, an ally of Austria-Hungary, declared war on Russia, Churchill predicted the Germans would soon invade Belgium in order to attack neighboring France.

He was right. On August 3, 1914, German troops advanced into Belgium, and twenty-four hours later, Britain was at war. As Churchill's navy protected the English Channel, which separates Britain from the European continent, 120,000 British soldiers were safely transported there within a few weeks.

At the outset of the Great War, later known as World War I (1914–1918), Churchill gave public speeches that inspired Britons, although he warned that the war would be long and somber. But when the enemy sank three British patrol cruisers, the public blamed him for the loss of these ships and the 1,459 men on board.

Churchill took great interest in the war on land, as well as at sea, and he set up a Royal Navy Division (RND) equipped to fight on land. He suggested that the best way to keep the ports along the channel open was to help the tiny Belgian army defend the fortress city of Antwerp, which guarded an arm of the sea. With the Germans at the edge of the city, Churchill arrived in Antwerp, along with a brigade of RND troops. He stayed in the city's finest hotel, issuing orders and messages from bed each morning, and toured the city's defenses wearing a cape and yachting cap.

But even with eight thousand British reinforcements, the Belgians could not hold off sixty thousand German

Belgian soldiers retreat from a massive German offensive on Antwerp in 1914. Although supported by the British military, the Belgians were unable to hold the city and their country.

troops. The city surrendered, and the RND withdrew to Dunkirk, on the French coast. Churchill was very depressed by the mission's failure and even considered resigning. The Conservatives criticized him for thinking his troops could have saved Antwerp and for his flashy style during the mission—which they called the Antwerp blunder. Nevertheless, a small strip of coastline in western Belgium, as well as the channel ports of France, remained out of German hands throughout the war.

Just as Churchill returned from Antwerp, on October 7, 1914, Clementine gave birth to their third child, Sarah. A few weeks later, Churchill turned forty and was named to the war cabinet, a small group of cabinet members that established war policies.

THE DARDANELLES

Although some people accused him of having a "lust for battle," Churchill sincerely wanted to find a way to shorten the war. By this time, troops on the western front, facing German troops to the east, were stuck in muddy trenches from the North Sea to the Swiss border.

With the western front at a stalemate, Churchill favored an attack on the Gallipoli Peninsula and the Dardanelles in Turkey, an ally of Germany. The Dardanelles is a narrow passage between the Mediterranean Sea and the Black Sea. Gaining control of the area would open the way to capturing Turkey's capital,

British soldiers make a land invasion at Gallipoli, Turkey, in 1915. The Turkish army soundly defeated the British along with their allies. Many blamed Churchill for the failure of the attack, and his political career suffered.

Constantinople, later renamed Istanbul. With Turkey out of the war, Britain could send supplies to allied Russian ports on the Black Sea and help the war on the eastern front.

British and French battleships launched a major attack on March 18, 1915. But the Turks had mobile guns on the cliffs overlooking the Dardanelles and set explosive mines in the water. After several ships sank, the Allied fleet retreated. In late April, Allied soldiers proceeded with a land attack on the Gallipoli Peninsula. It turned into a disaster. Over the next few months, hundreds of thousands of British, Australian, New Zealand, and French troops were killed.

Churchill had fought hard for the Dardanelles strategy in cabinet meetings, and many newspapers, political enemies, and the public blamed him for the failure of the campaign. It led to his immediate political downfall and haunted him for years.

To avoid a political crisis over the Dardanelles disaster, Liberal prime minister Herbert Asquith decided to form a coalition government with the Conservatives. The Conservatives agreed to join if Churchill was excluded from the cabinet. Churchill pleaded to stay, but Asquith fired him from the admiralty and offered him a position with no responsibilities, chancellor of the Duchy of Lancaster. Churchill reluctantly accepted so he could remain in the war cabinet.

The incident left Churchill deeply depressed and frustrated to be on the sidelines. Clementine later recalled, "When he left the Admiralty, he thought he was finished. I thought he would never get over the Dardanelles. I thought he would die of grief."

He could not stay idle for long. In the autumn, when it was clear that his former government colleagues were ignoring him, Churchill decided that, with his training as an officer, he could be of better use to his country with the troops. Wearing the uniform of a major with his old regiment, the Hussars, he crossed the channel. Once in France, he learned his way around the trenches with a crack regiment, the Second Battalion, Grenadier Guards. There, in the filthy, cold trenches, he felt happy and contented, even though he narrowly escaped death when a shell exploded in the trench where he had been sitting a few minutes earlier. Clementine sent him care packages that included brandy, cheese, and sardines. He also had a portable bath and hot water tank.

In January 1916, Churchill was appointed to command a battalion, the Sixth Royal Scots Fusiliers. The fusiliers (riflemen), mostly Scottish volunteers

CHURCHILL THE PAINTER

n the spring of 1915, Churchill and Clementine rented a country house in England with a pretty garden as a weekend retreat. One day Churchill watched his sister-in-law set up her easel and start to paint the scene. Intrigued, he asked an artist friend to get him started with oil paints, brushes, and canvas. At first, he hesitated, but once the friend demonstrated how to put the paint on the white canvas, Churchill recalled, "I seized the largest brush and fell upon my victim with berserk fury. I have never felt in awe of a canvas since."

Most of his paintings were landscapes, inspired by the sights he saw on his frequent travels through Europe. He became an accomplished amateur artist, but most of all, he found painting provided a wonderful way to get his mind off problems. He once told a friend, "If it weren't for painting, I couldn't live. I couldn't bear the strain of things."

rather than professional soldiers, soon came to respect him. He improved safety in the trenches, tried to eliminate the lice that infested unwashed bodies, organized entertainment, and raised the soldiers' morale. After several months, however, he concluded his true place was in Parliament, and he returned to England in May.

Asquith resigned and David Lloyd George replaced him as prime minister. A commission investigated the events at the Dardanelles and, in March 1917, issued a report that put no blame on Churchill. With that burden lifted from his shoulders, his depression eased and he became determined to return to public office.

Finally, in July 1917, despite the protests of the Conservatives, Lloyd George appointed Churchill minister of munitions, in charge of war supplies, although he left him out of the war cabinet. Russia had collapsed, German submarines were sinking British ships, and although the United States had declared war on Germany, it needed time to train and supply its troops. U.S. soldiers would not be ready to fight until 1918.

When the Germans launched a successful offensive against France in the spring of 1918, Churchill toured the front lines with French prime minister Georges Clemenceau. But by autumn, the tide had turned against the Germans, partly because of the success of the new British invention, the tank. The tank is an armored vehicle that can travel in all kinds of terrain. Churchill had been an enthusiastic supporter of the development of the tank since the beginning of the war, and he contributed ideas on strategic ways to use it in battle. In addition, U.S. soldiers had finally arrived to help drive back the enemy. Churchill was able to produce the needed armaments and supplies, including airplanes and poisonous mustard gas. First, Austria-Hungary surrendered, then Germany, and the guns were silenced on November 11, 1918. The Treaty of Versailles formally ended World War I the next year.

SECRETARY OF STATE FOR WAR AND AIR

In Britain Lloyd George called a general election for early December. No one party won a majority of seats in Parliament, so another coalition government was led by Lloyd George. He named Churchill secretary of state for war and air.

In this position, Churchill kept busy over the next few years with a series of international issues, including the reparations (payment for damages) the Germans had to make following the war. Churchill was one of the few members of the coalition government who did not believe in being too hard on the defeated nation.

In Russia the Bolsheviks (Communists) had led a revolution and come to power in 1917. Armed opponents were still resisting them in 1919. Churchill said, "Of all the tyrannies in history, the Bolshevik tyranny is the worst, the most destructive, the most degrading." Britain still had arms and troops in northern Russia at the end of the war, and Churchill was at the center of discussions as to whether Britain should help the anti-Bolshevik forces. He supported the idea, but by the end of 1919, a combination of factors, including military failures and opposition in Britain, forced him to order the British troops to evacuate.

In 1921 Churchill changed cabinet posts and took on the colonial office. There, his responsibilities included trying to control the costs of running Britain's colonies in the Middle East, including Iraq, Arabia, and Palestine. Churchill strongly supported the establishment of a Jewish state in Palestine. He traveled to the Middle East and, over the next year, helped to make the government's Palestine policy a reality. Part of this policy was the establishment of a homeland for the Jews, who were scattered all over the world.

Churchill had worries at home too. In the spring of that year, his mother broke her ankle. It became infected, and her leg was amputated. She seemed to be getting better, but then she suffered sudden bleeding. She died on June 26, 1921, her son at her bedside. Although she had been married and divorced twice since Lord Randolph's death, she was buried next to him. Churchill wrote a friend, "I do not feel a sense of tragedy, but only of loss. Her life was a full one."

But tragedy did affect the family in August when their youngest child, Marigold, died of meningitis at the age of two. Churchill and Clementine were devastated, but while she stayed in London to be near the baby's grave, he went to Scotland to paint in solitude.

THE IRISH TREATY

On his return to London, Churchill took part in negotiations over the future of Ireland. Many Irish people,
especially those in the primarily Roman Catholic
south, wanted Ireland to be independent, rather than
part of the United Kingdom of Great Britain and Ireland. Terrorist acts and killings had increased to the
point that the Irish Republican Army (IRA) was at
war with the British army.

In 1921 Churchill and several other British representatives held a series of meetings with negotiators

*Irish delegates sign the Anglo-Irish Treaty in December 1921.
Churchill helped broker the treaty—which established Northern
Ireland and the independent Republic of Ireland—in hopes of
bringing an end to violence there.*

for Sinn Fein, the IRA's political party, to try to end the bloodshed. Churchill proposed an agreement that would give the South the status of an Irish state, while Ulster, the heavily Protestant region in the North, could remain part of the United Kingdom. The Anglo-Irish Treaty was signed in early December, and Churchill was instrumental in persuading Parliament to approve it. In Ireland, however, the violence continued.

In 1922 several important events occurred in Churchill's personal life. He had recently inherited a property in Ireland from a distant relative. The rental income helped relieve his constant shortage of cash, although it did not decrease his carefree spending habits. Without consulting Clementine, he used some of that income, along with some of the proceeds from sales of his books, to buy Chartwell, a country house in Kent. On the same day, Mary, the couple's fifth and last child, was born.

In October the Conservatives withdrew their support from the coalition government. According to British government laws, if the prime minister doesn't control a majority of Parliament, the prime minister has to resign and call for new elections. Lloyd George had to resign. Churchill, who had just had his appendix removed, lost his seat in the election that followed. He noted, "In the twinkling of an eye, I found myself without an office, without a seat, without a party, and without an appendix."

Winston Churchill in 1922. That year British voters ousted him from Parliament during the general election.

Chapter **FOUR**

THE WILDERNESS YEARS

CHURCHILL'S LIFE WAS LIKE A ROLLER COASTER, WITH thrilling ups and many downs. When the general election of 1922 took him down to defeat, it was the first time in twenty-two years that he was without a seat in Parliament. He was busy with a major writing project, however, the first book of a five-volume set about the Great War, entitled *The World Crisis*.

In Britain power swung back and forth between the political parties. For a time, the Labour Party formed the government. Churchill disliked Labour, partly because many of its supporters sympathized with the Bolsheviks in Russia.

It seemed clear that the once-powerful Liberals had lost public support, and he decided the only party that

Churchill argues the Conservative cause to citizens in Epping, England, during the 1924 general election campaign.

could effectively oppose Labour was the Conservatives, so Churchill switched parties again. Following the general election of 1924, the new Conservative prime minister, Stanley Baldwin, invited Churchill to be chancellor of the exchequer, the post Lord Randolph had once held. Shortly after taking office, Churchill celebrated his fiftieth birthday.

Churchill had a hard time with his personal finances, but he threw himself into this new challenge of running Britain's finances with his usual enthusiasm. As chancellor, he renewed his interest in social reform and introduced pensions for widows and orphans. He held the post for more than four years and presented five budgets, each time with a speech that was longer and more entertaining than the last.

THE GENERAL STRIKE

The policies he introduced in his first budget (in 1925) were based on the advice of bankers and economists in his department. The policies caused the prices of goods that Britain exported to rise, so people in other countries bought fewer British products. This damaged the British economy. The coal industry, which employed a million people, was particularly hard hit by the economic slump. The coal miners went on strike in the summer of 1926 to protest the mine owners' demands to cut their pay. In sympathy, workers in all industries went out on a nine-day, nationwide general strike.

Newspapers joined the strike in this pretelevision era, so rather than have rumors circulate around the country, Churchill rolled up his sleeves and supervised the production of an official government publication, the *British Gazette*. After the general strike ended, he took part in the negotiations to end the coal strike.

In 1927 and 1928, Churchill spent a lot of time at Chartwell. He supervised the construction of ponds and dams on the property. Since he enjoyed bricklaying, he helped to put up brick walls around the gardens and to build a small cottage for young Mary. He also painted a great deal and worked on his books.

LIFE AT CHARTWELL

Chartwell, a sturdy old English manor house in the countryside near London, is surrounded by butterfly-filled flower gardens, a terraced lawn, and ponds. Clementine worried about the costs of maintaining it, but Churchill, who had always managed somehow to live beyond his means, was not concerned. For him, Chartwell became a haven, especially during the difficult years between the two world wars.

During that period, he was a loving and indulgent family man. Each family member had a nickname: he and Clemmie called each other Cat and Pug, Diana was Puppy Kitten, Randolph was the Chumbelly, stubborn Sarah was Mule, and Mary was Mouse. The children called him Pa-PAH. He was a great animal lover, and several dogs and cats lived in the household.

Eighteen servants kept Chartwell and Churchill running. There were maids to clean and serve meals, secretaries who wrote down Churchill's dictations and typed them up, and Churchill's "man," or valet, who helped him with all his personal needs, from running his bath to tying his tie. Churchill was a difficult boss, however. He often went into a rage when someone made a mistake, and he never apologized for his rudeness.

Churchill had an unwavering routine. He slept deeply, a mask covering his eyes to ensure darkness. When he woke up, his valet brought breakfast, including orange juice, a piece of leftover meat from dinner, and a dish of jam. After his bath, he put on his dressing gown. Then, while sipping on a scotch and soda and chewing on a cigar, he read the morning newspapers and the mail and began to dictate a speech or give instructions to a research assistant.

His many writings—books, newspaper columns, and magazine articles—provided the bulk of his income. Although his distinctive writing style and controversial opinions made him hugely popular, he relied on badly paid researchers to prepare the background for his books and articles.

After lunch Churchill fed the fish, ducks, and black swans in the ponds, and then he just sat alone and thought for a while. He sometimes did some painting in his studio, and he always took an afternoon nap, often sleeping for two hours. Then he played cards in the living room with Clemmie until about seven, when he went upstairs for another bath. He liked to play and splash in the bath, and he often summoned a secretary to take dictation or invited a friend to come and talk while he washed. More than one acquaintance got an unexpected view of his round, pink, naked frame, but Churchill did not seem to mind.

Dinner was scheduled for eight thirty, and there were nearly always guests. The meal was the main event of the day and not just for the menu, which might include soup, trout, roast beef, and chocolate eclairs, as well as champagne, brandy, and cigars. For Churchill, the conversation was the highlight of the meal, "with myself as chief conversationalist." (Although he enjoyed his guests' amusing remarks, he was not in the least interested in their opinions.

Finally, at about eleven o'clock, Churchill said good night to his guests and, putting on his red, green and gold dressing gown, began his most productive time of the day. He usually worked until three or four in the morning, dictating several thousand words of an article, revising typed drafts, and transforming the research provided by his assistants. His memory and his ability to concentrate on his work were phenomenal.

Whenever he wrote a speech, he polished every word and gave himself stage directions—to pause or to correct himself, for example—so that the speech would appear spontaneous. (He was never good at speaking without a prepared text.) He was often genuinely affected by his own words and even wept in public as he delivered moving passages or when he was touched by things he saw or heard.

The election of 1929 brought the Labour Party to power, although Churchill retained his own Conservative seat. He busied himself with magazine articles and plans for a biography of his famous ancestor, the first Duke of Marlborough.

That summer Churchill, his son Randolph, and his brother Jack toured North America. They crossed Canada in a special railway car, and Churchill made speeches along the way. In California he met actor Charlie Chaplin and stayed with multimillionaire newspaper owner William Randolph Hearst. He was in New York City on October 24, 1929, the day the stock market crashed. He lost a substantial amount of money in the crash. The market crash eventually led to a worldwide economic depression. Churchill's own finances improved when *My Early Life,* his autobiography of his childhood and youth, was released in 1930 and became an international best-seller.

The new Labour government proposed granting the British colony of India a step toward independence. Churchill strongly opposed the idea and joined the debate in 1930 to 1931. He felt that there were too many divisions between the two major religious groups in India, the Hindus and Muslims. He warned that if India achieved independence too quickly, the conflicts between Hindus and Muslims would quickly destroy the peace and prosperity British rule had provided. But the leaders of both the Conservative and Labour parties were committed to India's independence.

This British political poster urges voters to elect members of the coalition National Government Party to Parliament during the 1931 general election. Churchill, and other members of the coalition party, won a majority vote.

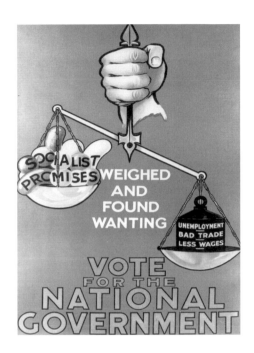

Churchill was on the losing side of this important issue, and as a result, his Conservative colleagues cut him out of the influential inner circle of the party. In the autumn of 1931, economic troubles brought down the Labour government, and the British people voted for a new all-party coalition government. Churchill won his seat, but was not offered a cabinet position. He called this period when he was excluded from power or influence his "wilderness years."

Free of government duties except his seat in the House, he arranged a well-paying lecture tour of the United States, accompanied by Clementine and Diana.

On their first stop, New York City, Churchill forgot that cars drive on the right in the United States, rather than on the left, as in Britain, and he was accidentally hit by a car. While recovering from his injuries, he caught paratyphoid, a bacterial disease that causes fever and intestinal problems. After a slow recovery, he resumed the tour in January 1932. When he arrived back in London in March, several friends gave him a luxury car to celebrate his recovery.

THE NAZI THREAT

Although he was back in Britain, he was still excluded from the inner circle of decision makers. At that time, the rise of Adolf Hitler and his Nazi Party in Germany became an issue for Churchill. But he had little influence in the government, and the vast majority of Britons saw no problem.

Britain failed to acknowledge the danger posed by the Nazis for a number of reasons. During the first World War, about 1.2 million soldiers from Britain and its empire were killed in action and 2 million were wounded. Germany and its allies lost 3 million people, with 8 million wounded. When people saw these numbers, they were horrified by the suffering and waste of human life. Pacifism (a peace movement) was at its height in Britain in the 1930s.

Also, the Treaty of Versailles had imposed severe punishment on Germany. The victors forced Germany to pay $31.5 billion to the Allies for the costs they had incurred during the war. The treaty limited Germany's armed forces to one hundred thousand men, a few navy ships, and no aircraft. A demilitarized zone (where arms were prohibited) called the Rhineland was established between Germany and Belgium and France. Located on the banks of the Rhine River, it included several large cities with primarily German-speaking inhabitants.

By the early 1930s, many people felt that the Versailles Treaty had been too hard on Germany. Placing all the blame on the losers seemed unfair, especially in light of the huge profits that arms manufacturers had made during the war. Some people also realized that the humiliating treaty would cause some Germans to yearn for revenge. This was a frightening thought, since Germany had both a large population and a strategic location in the middle of Europe.

The fear of Communism was also a factor. During the 1930s, the Soviet Union (formerly the Russian Empire) was under the control of the dictator Joseph Stalin, who murdered his opponents or sent them to die in concentrations camps. Stalin seemed to want to undermine European governments and encourage Communist revolutions everywhere.

In Britain Communism—which in theory gave power to the working people, rather than the rich and powerful—had become fashionable among students and intellectuals. A growing number of working-class Britons also sympathized with Communism, especially after the depression during the 1930s left nearly one-quarter of the country's workforce unemployed. Many worried Conservatives saw Germany as protection against the Communist threat. Finally, many citizens and government leaders simply refused to believe anything bad they heard about Germany or to even think about the possibility of another war.

Initially, the Nazi Party had few followers. But the economic chaos of the depression changed that, and by 1932, it had become a leading political party in

Adolf Hitler, standing in car, *salutes his storm troopers, the SS. These loyal soldiers used force to make sure Hitler remained in power.*

Germany. After Nazi leader Adolf Hitler was sworn in as chancellor (national leader) in January 1933, he moved quickly. His storm troopers dragged critics off to be beaten and tortured. Before the end of March, the German parliament passed an act making Hitler a dictator, a leader with absolute power.

Hitler convinced Germans that they belonged to a superior northern European race. He ordered Jews, Communists, members of various minority groups, as well as critics of Nazi policies to be rounded up and sent to concentration camps. Intellectuals, writers, artists, and scientists who disagreed with Hitler's policies fled. Young boys were trained in military skills, and in a huge effort to re-arm, the country built factories that made arms, airplanes, and spare parts, in defiance of the Treaty of Versailles.

In Britain Churchill was one of a very few voices to sound an alarm. He argued that Britain must arm itself. Otherwise its military weakness would invite attack. Many people distrusted Churchill. Some even disliked him intensely. Newspapers published his articles, and people still admired his wit and energy. But they felt he was out of tune with the times when he talked of the need for arms rather than disarmament.

He repeatedly spoke in Parliament of his concerns about Germany, but other members ignored him or left the chamber when he rose to speak. In the coalition government, Labour Party members were pledged to pacifism, and the Conservatives were committed to appeasement, or achieving peace by meeting Hitler's demands. Moreover, based on his opposition to independence for India (the India Bill was finally approved in 1935), many members of Parliament (MPs) questioned Churchill's judgment. Even many of his old friends thought Churchill misjudged the Nazis.

"MOST SECRET" INFORMATION

A few British journalists, diplomats, and others who visited Germany during the 1930s did notice what was going on there. When government officials ignored their reports or claimed they were untrue, a number of these documents—including many labeled "most secret"—ended up on Churchill's desk at Chartwell. Among Churchill's informants were several key civil servants and intelligence officials who risked their own careers to supply him with information about the German arms buildup and the weakness of the British military defenses.

Churchill pressed particularly hard on the issue of air strength. In 1934 he warned that the German air force would be almost double the size of the Britain's Royal Air Force (RAF) within three years. Newer planes could cover long distances, flying at speeds of more than two hundred miles an hour. He reminded Britons that they could not retreat from an air attack—they could not move London. The prime minister insisted the RAF was far superior to German air power and pledged that it would remain so.

German soldiers on the march during the 1930s. Churchill was suspicious of Hitler, believing that the dictator had nothing but ominous plans for Europe. But few would listen to him.

In 1935 Hitler introduced compulsory military service in Germany. With every young man trained in the military, he could easily double or triple the size of his armed forces. In the British general election later that year, the Conservatives won a huge victory. Churchill hoped his differences with Prime Minister Stanley Baldwin were forgotten and that he would be offered a cabinet post. He sat by the phone for six days, but it never rang. Frustrated and depressed, he and Clementine went to France and Morocco for a holiday.

In 1936 German troops marched into the Rhineland. Hitler bet that France and its allies would do nothing in response, and he was right. Meanwhile, he promised to work toward an understanding with his European neighbors. While most Britons believed him, Churchill did not. In fact, Churchill had come to believe that, whatever Hitler said, the opposite was true.

Churchill spoke of the importance of respect for international treaty agreements. Meanwhile, he was trying hard to get himself back into the cabinet, where he could have greater influence. Even while Churchill was not in an important political office, however, Hitler knew of his reputation and hated him.

After the invasion of the Rhineland, Baldwin created a new ministry for the coordination of defense. Many people thought Churchill the obvious man to be the new minister, but Baldwin worried that if he picked Churchill, Hitler would be angry. Instead, the prime minister appointed a little-known lawyer with no military experience. This came as a bitter blow to Churchill, although he tried to hide his feelings.

Over the next few years, the new department made little progress in improving defenses and increasing arms production, and Churchill accused it of wasting time, "drifting and dawdling as the precious months flow out." In 1936 Chancellor of the Exchequer Neville Chamberlain turned down Churchill's suggestion that factories be compelled to make war materials, saying he did not want to disturb the peacetime economy.

In the fall of 1936, Churchill was distracted by family matters. His daughter Sarah was his favorite, and he had always given her whatever she wanted. Now an aspiring actress, she wanted to marry a comedian who had been married twice before. At first, Churchill opposed the marriage, so the couple went to the United States. Eventually Churchill gave the couple his blessing, and they were married.

Meanwhile, Churchill continued to try to raise public awareness of the looming danger and need for military preparations through speeches in the House and through his newspaper columns, which were published in about fourteen countries. Government leaders continued to think that negotiations could avoid war. They dismissed Churchill as an alarmist and accused him of trying to stir up trouble. They did not think anyone, including Hitler, wanted another conflict. But Churchill seemed to understand Hitler, perhaps because he had such an aggressive personality himself.

Finally, he felt he was making progress, and he addressed a large rally of people who favored rearming the country. Then an issue arose that not only distracted the public and politicians but destroyed Churchill's credibility again. That issue was the abdication crisis.

THE ABDICATION CRISIS

King Edward VIII, a forty-two-year-old bachelor, had fallen in love with Wallis Simpson, a divorced American who was still married to her second husband.

It was clear to many, including Churchill, that a divorced American could never be accepted as queen. Prime Minister Baldwin gave Edward a choice: give up Wallis Simpson or abdicate (give up the crown) and be succeeded by his brother. Edward chose to abdicate, and most Britons seemed to agree this was the best course.

Churchill was a loyal and romantic believer in the crown, and he wanted to give the king more time to reconsider. But when he rose in the House of Commons to speak on this subject, the other members shouted him down. They thought he was trying to make more trouble for the government. He had misjudged public opinion and left the House humiliated. After that, it seemed, his political career was over, and what he called his "black dog"—bouts of depression—returned.

Churchill faced financial as well as political problems. Chartwell was expensive, and the children had grown up. He considered selling the estate, but a friend helped with a loan. This difficulty resolved, Churchill focused on writing the fourth and final volume of the Duke of Marlborough biography. Publicly, he spoke of the increasingly serious persecution of the Jews in Germany, but the issue was not taken very seriously in Great Britain, where anti-Semitism was common.

In 1937 Stanley Baldwin retired, and Neville Chamberlain became prime minister. He and Churchill had

British prime minister Neville Chamberlain, left, *shakes hands with Adolf Hitler during the Munich Conference in 1938. Chamberlain believed that allowing Hitler to take the Sudetenland would bring lasting peace to Europe. Churchill believed otherwise.*

never gotten along. And like Baldwin, Chamberlain believed that by appeasing Hitler and giving him what he wanted, he could prevent war with Nazi Germany.

Early in 1938, Hitler's troops moved again, this time taking control of neighboring Austria. It looked like democratic Czechoslovakia would be next. Hitler wanted the Sudetenland, a part of Czechoslovakia with a large population of German descent.

In September Chamberlain attended a meeting in Munich with Hitler, Italian dictator Benito Mussolini, and Édouard Daladier, the prime minister of France. The leaders agreed to allow Germany to occupy the Sudetenland. They hoped once again this would avoid war. Churchill, of course, voiced his doubts.

About Christmastime 1938, a bright spot appeared in the Churchill family. Diana, married to Duncan Sandys, a young Conservative member of Parliament, gave birth to Churchill's first granddaughter. Early in the new year, Churchill visited friends in France. After he had left, his friend wrote to him, "We rocked with laughter continually. Your *joie de vivre* [joy for life] is a wonderful gift ... in fact you are the most enormously gifted creature in the whole world, and it is like sunshine leaving when you go away."

But in March, there was no time for laughter. German troops crossed into Czechoslovakia and took control of the country. Finally alarmed, Prime Minister Chamberlain promised to help Poland if the Germans

A German tank division receives honors for its participation in the capture of Poland in 1939. With the German invasion of Poland, Britain—allied with Poland—was at war.

attacked it. A few weeks later, the British government followed Churchill's advice of three years earlier and established a ministry of supply that would oversee the production of war materials. Soon newspaper editorials began demanding Churchill's inclusion in the cabinet, but Churchill was still at Chartwell, working on a new book project, *History of the English-Speaking Peoples*.

At the end of August, Britain signed a formal Treaty of Alliance with Poland. On September 1, 1939, Hitler's armies invaded Poland. Churchill's secretary later recalled that her boss "paced up and down like a lion in a cage. He was expecting a call (inviting him to join the war cabinet) but the call never came." On September 3, 1939, after Hitler failed to reply to British demands for withdrawal from Poland, Britain declared war on Germany. World War II had begun.

First lord of the admiralty Winston Churchill, front, *inspects a secret British military base in 1939.*

Chapter FIVE

WORLD WAR II: HIS FINEST HOUR

CHURCHILL LISTENED ON THE RADIO AS PRIME MINISTER Chamberlain announced that Britain was at war. Later that day, Chamberlain named Churchill to his former post, first lord of the admiralty, and to a place in the war cabinet. Upon the news, the admiralty head office sent a message to all navy ships, "Winston is back." Six days later, Churchill's warships began escorting the first British troops to France, just as in 1914.

Churchill took time out in October to attend Randolph's wedding. When some friends expressed concern that the young couple did not have much money, Churchill replied, "What do they need?—cigars, champagne and a double bed." A few weeks later, Churchill celebrated his own sixty-fifth birthday.

Britain lost its first major campaign in the war, a naval battle to prevent the Germans from occupying Norway. In Britain, frustration with the country's leadership grew, and people felt it was time for a change. Many members of Parliament believed that Churchill had the energy to tackle the huge task and that Britons were ready to follow him. On May 10, 1940, Chamberlain resigned and Churchill became prime minister. On the same day, German forces drove into Holland, Belgium, and France.

Churchill later recalled that, despite the bad news from the war front, at the end of that day, he felt "a profound sense of relief. At last I had authority to give directions over the whole scene. I felt as if I were walking with destiny, and that all my past life had been but a preparation for this hour and for this trial."

In France, the Germans had isolated the British forces and threatened to cut them off from the coast, so they couldn't escape across the channel to England. Churchill ordered the British forces to march to the French coastal town of Dunkirk. From there, under German air attack, more than 224,000 British and 111,000 French soldiers were transported to England by fishing boats, pleasure boats, and paddle steamers. Churchill ordered troops at nearby Calais, France, to stay and hold off the Germans to protect the evacuation at Dunkirk.

Some cabinet ministers still wanted to negotiate with the Germans, but Churchill held firm. On June

British and French troops evacuate Dunkirk, France, for the safety of England, escaping an advancing German military in 1940.

4, the day after the evacuation ended, he addressed the House of Commons with one of his most famous wartime speeches. He vowed:

> We shall go on to the end. We shall fight in France, we shall fight in the seas and oceans, we shall fight with growing confidence and growing strengths in the air, we shall defend our island, whatever the cost may be. We shall fight on the beaches, we shall fight on the landing grounds, we shall fight in the fields and in the streets, we shall fight in the hills; we shall never surrender.

This British poster from World War II shows Churchill as a determined, unflinching bulldog. Despite the retreat at Dunkirk, France, and relentless German air attacks on Britain, Churchill promised that the British would not give up the fight.

HOLDING THE LINE!

A week later, Italy declared war on Britain and France, and French government leaders evacuated Paris. On June 16, France asked Germany for an end to the fighting, and Britain was left to oppose Germany, essentially alone. A few days later, Churchill made another difficult decision: to destroy several French warships so they would not fall into German hands.

THE BATTLE OF BRITAIN

As Churchill had predicted, the major threat to Britain came from the air. Although the British produced more than 350 aircraft a week, the enemy shot them down almost as fast as they were manufactured. In late June, the Battle of Britain began, as wave after wave of German bombers and fighter aircraft attacked British docks, factories, and cities. Over the next few months, thousands of civilians were killed in London and other British cities. Every day for twelve days in late August, 600 planes a day attacked English cities and airports.

At the most critical point of the battle, Britain had no more reserves left. If another wave of enemy aircraft had arrived, the British defenses would have crumbled. But it didn't, and by mid-September, the British had been able to destroy enough German planes to turn the tide of the battle.

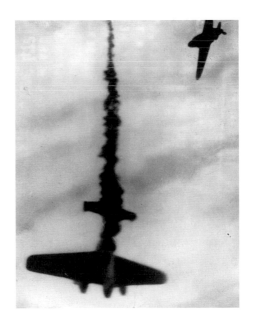

The pilot of a British Hurricane, top right, *shoots down a German Messerschmitt fighter plane over Sussex, England, during the Battle of Britain.*

WARTIME WORDS

Churchill gave his most famous speech, later called the "Their Finest Hour" speech, to the House of Commons, on June 18, 1940, on the eve of the Battle of Britain.

Upon this battle depends the survival of Christian civilization. Upon it depends our own British life, and the long continuity of our institutions and our Empire. The whole fury and might of the enemy must very soon be turned on us. Hitler knows that he will have to break us in this island or lose the war. If we can stand up to him, all Europe may be free and the life of the world may move forward into broad, sunlit uplands. But if we fail, then the whole world, including the United States, including all that we have known and cared for, will sink into the abyss of a new Dark Age made more sinister, and perhaps more protracted, by the lights of perverted science. Let us therefore brace ourselves to our duties and so bear ourselves that, if the British Empire and its Commonwealth last for a thousand years, men will still say, "This was their finest hour."

In an address to the students of Harrow, his old school, in 1941, Churchill said: "[S]urely from this period of ten months, this is the lesson: never give in, never give in, never, never, never, never—in nothing, great or small, large or petty—never give in except to convictions of honor and good sense."

The inscription in his six-volume memoir *The Second World War* expresses his philosophy: "In war, Resolution. In defeat, Defiance. In victory, Magnanimity. In peace, Goodwill."

Churchill paid homage to the British pilots who defended their homeland. He gratefully stated, "Never in the field of human conflict has so much been owed by so many to so few."

Nevertheless, Churchill was still worried that Hitler planned to invade Britain. He was relieved to learn from intercepted German messages that this was unlikely. One of Churchill's greatest military advantages during the war was the ability to eavesdrop on top-secret enemy radio messages, including orders, reports, and locations. Code breakers at Bletchley Park, the Government Code and Cypher School near London, unraveled these messages and delivered them daily to the prime minister's desk.

The British used these messages to avoid the threat that now came from the sea. German submarines were sinking merchant (supply) ships at an alarming rate. The merchant ships ferried food and war supplies from North America to Britain. After victory in the Battle of Britain was assured, the Battle of the Atlantic became a top priority.

Churchill did not stay in the prime minister's usual residence at 10 Downing Street. Working from steel-fortified offices and living quarters known as No. 10 Annexe and the nearby underground Central War Rooms, Churchill drove himself hard. He issued urgent notes to his staff, tagged with red stickers marked "action this day." He was a fountain of energy and ideas, although his staff had to disagree with his wilder suggestions. His military chief of staff later observed that Churchill had ten ideas a day, one good, nine bad. With so much responsibility resting on his shoulders, the stress took a toll. Clementine warned her husband that "there is a danger of your being generally disliked by your colleagues and subordinates because of your rough sarcastic and overbearing manner."

CHURCHILL AND ROOSEVELT

Churchill had always felt strong ties with the United States, and he was convinced that President Franklin D. Roosevelt would help. Churchill appealed to the U.S. president and kept him informed of developments. Roosevelt, however, was reluctant to take the United States into this European conflict. In the summer of 1940, Roosevelt secretly agreed that the United States would manufacture aircraft and weapons for Britain and lease (rent) it several destroyers. In return, the British allowed the United States to use its naval bases in Newfoundland, Canada, and in the West Indies for ships to protect the U.S. coastline.

By the end of 1940, Britain was having difficulty paying for these war supplies. Roosevelt sent an adviser named Harry Hopkins to Britain to discuss the situation, and Hopkins and Churchill became friends. They worked out a deal called the Lend-Lease Agreement. The United States would build tanks and other equipment and lease them to Britain. Britain would pay all it could immediately, then repay the remaining debt after the war. In a radio broadcast, Churchill spoke of the mighty tide of friendship and aid that had begun to flow across the Atlantic. He told Roosevelt that if the United States gave Britain the tools that it needed, Britain would defeat Hitler.

By then the war raged in North Africa and the Mediterranean region. The German air raids on Britain also continued, and by April 1941, the civilian death toll had reached thirty thousand. In retaliation, British bombers flew missions to attack German targets.

Tanks roll off an assembly line in Detroit, Michigan, in 1940. Many of these tanks were part of the Lend-Lease program and were bound for Britain.

But Churchill's strongest weapons were his words. U.S. war correspondent Edward R. Murrow observed that one of Churchill's greatest achievements was that he "mobilized the English language and sent it into battle."

Churchill deliberately developed a strong public image, which was caught in newspaper photos and newsreels (short news films shown in theaters with the feature films). His stout figure, a cigar clamped in his mouth, and his fingers forming a *V* for victory became a familiar sight. He usually wore a zippered overall called a siren suit, which he ordered made in various types of fabric for different occasions. He was also known for having a drink at his side, although he never appeared drunk.

When Churchill woke up on June 22, 1941, he learned that Germany had invaded Russia. For him, this was actually good news, since Britain needed a powerful ally. Although he had always hated Bolshevism, he pledged that "any man or state who fights against Nazism will have our aid." Churchill supplied Stalin with tanks and secret information, gathered at Bletchley, about German war plans.

In August Churchill sailed on the battleship *Prince of Wales* to Placentia Bay, Newfoundland, to meet secretly with Roosevelt aboard the USS *Augusta*. The crews of the two vessels held a joint church service, singing rousing hymns chosen by Churchill, and he turned on all his charm for the U.S. president. The two leaders signed the Atlantic Charter, committing both countries to democratic ideals and issuing a warning to Japan to halt its expansion into countries in Southeast Asia. But Churchill was disappointed that the United States seemed no closer to joining the war.

THE UNITED STATES JOINS THE WAR

On December 7, 1941, Japanese aircraft attacked U.S. ships at Pearl Harbor, Hawaii. The United States immediately declared war on Japan. A few days later, Italy and Germany declared war on the United States.

A U.S. artillery unit shells a German position in 1942. The United States had joined the war the previous year.

Finally, this crucial ally of Great Britain had fully joined the war. Churchill crossed the Atlantic again, arriving at the White House just before Christmas. He and Roosevelt made a key agreement to defeat Germany before defeating Japan.

While in Washington, Churchill felt a pain in his chest. Churchill's doctor realized the prime minister had suffered a mild heart attack. He told no one, however, not even the patient. He was concerned that morale would suffer if the truth became public. So Churchill continued with his planned schedule, visiting Ottawa, Canada, then resting in Florida and Bermuda before flying back to Great Britain.

In February 1942, the terrible news came that Singapore, a British colony in Southeast Asia, had fallen to the Japanese. Meanwhile, German submarines continued to take a huge toll on Allied ships. Growing numbers of Britons criticized Churchill's leadership. "He is not too well physically, and he is worn down by the continuous crushing pressure of events," his daughter Mary noted.

In June he returned to the United States to discuss strategy. Churchill and Roosevelt agreed that they were not yet ready to send a large invasion force across the channel. Instead, they would concentrate on the war in the Atlantic and North Africa. They also secretly agreed to share research into the development of an atom bomb.

A month later, Churchill traveled to the desert in

North Africa. The British had recently suffered a disastrous defeat there at Tobruk, Libya. Then Churchill went on to Cairo, Egypt, where he spent nine days talking to the men and officers in order to improve morale. He also replaced the top military commander in the region.

From Cairo Churchill flew to Moscow to get to know Stalin personally. Stalin criticized Churchill for the lack of progress in western Europe. He was anxious for the Allies to send an invasion force across the channel because it might force the Germans to withdraw from the Russian front. Churchill told him that was impossible in 1942 but promised increased bombing of German cities. Churchill said that Britain looked on the morale of German civilians as a military target. "We sought no mercy and we would show no mercy."

In August Canadian troops landed on the beaches of Dieppe, France, in a quick raid that was supposed to make the Germans think a full-scale invasion was coming. The raid was badly planned, the troops were poorly trained, and they did not have sufficient firepower. Several thousand Canadians were killed or taken prisoner, but Allied commanders learned valuable lessons from the experience.

THE END OF THE BEGINNING

The Allies began an attack on German-Italian forces at El Alamein, Egypt, in October. Their victory was a turning point in the war, and Churchill ordered bells rung throughout England to celebrate. However, he cautioned, "Now this is not the end. It is not even the beginning of the end. But it is, perhaps, the end of the beginning."

In January 1943, Churchill flew to Casablanca, Morocco, to meet with Roosevelt. After their official meetings, they drove together to the Moroccan city of Marrakech. Churchill remembered having spent a pleasant visit there before the war, and he wanted to show Roosevelt the view of the sunset over the snow-capped Atlas Mountains. After Roosevelt left, Churchill stayed there alone for another day to paint. It was the only painting he did during the war. Upon his return to Great Britain, he came down with pneumonia and was in bed for a week.

Churchill traveled to Washington, D.C., again in May to discuss strategy for the offensive against the enemy. He and the U.S. president also agreed that their scientists would work together to manufacture an atom bomb. On his way back to Europe, Churchill visited Supreme Allied Commander General Dwight D. Eisenhower's headquarters in Algiers, Algeria. That summer Eisenhower's forces landed in Sicily, the first step toward an invasion of Italy.

In Quebec City, Canada, in August, Churchill met with Canadian and U.S. leaders. Then, after a few days fishing in Canada's Laurentian Mountains, Churchill went to Washington for more talks with the president and to Boston, Massachusetts, where he received an honorary degree from Harvard University. By the time he reached home, he had traveled 111,000 miles by sea and air in the preceding five years.

He was off again in November to Tehran, Iran, for the first meeting of the Big Three—Churchill, Roosevelt, and Stalin. By this time, Churchill was physically weak and Britain was struggling. Its economy had been hurt by the long conflict, and its armed forces could no longer win battles without help. Churchill was unable to persuade the others to do things his way. The United States had become the strongest military power, and Russia also remained strong, so their leaders controlled the Big Three.

Churchill was concerned about how Europe would look after the war. He worried that Stalin would push the boundaries of the Soviet Union as far west as possible, thus dividing Europe into a Communist-influenced East and a democratic West. The Americans, however, were just interested in winning the war.

After the Tehran conference, Churchill flew to Carthage, Tunisia. He developed a fever, and the doctor diagnosed pneumonia. In addition, he suffered two more mild heart attacks. Clementine traveled to North Africa to join him, and they spent Christmas there. He soon started to feel better, however, dictating messages, meeting with Allied commanders in his dragon-decorated dressing gown, and smoking cigars again. He returned to London in mid-January.

D-Day

During the early months of 1944, Churchill and the Allied commanders prepared for Operation Overlord, the name given to the D-day invasion of occupied France. But everyone noticed how tired Churchill was. He seemed unable to concentrate and rambled on during meetings.

He also came under criticism in the House of Commons for the heavy Allied bombing of German cities and the deaths of thousands of German civilians. He defended his actions, saying that both Germany and Japan were the nations that had selected airpower as their main weapon. But a few months later, while watching a film of the devastating effects of the bombings, he burst out, "Are we beasts? Have we taken this too far?"

On D-day, June 6, 1944, Allied troops fought their way onto the beaches of Normandy on the French coast. In retaliation, the Germans sent a new weapon, rocket-propelled bombs, across the channel to London. Nevertheless, more than five hundred thousand Allied troops were soon in France, and the invasion became an overwhelming success. On August 24, the Allies entered Paris and the Germans were retreating. These victories gave Churchill a huge boost, and he felt so energetic that he went to observe the fighting firsthand in France and Italy during the summer.

Meanwhile, Russian troops scored a huge victory on the eastern front. Churchill hoped to keep Greece

Allied soldiers make their way onto Omaha Beach during the D-day invasion of German-occupied France in June 1944.

from falling under Communism, and he still hoped that Poland could have a democratic, independent future. He was on the road again in the fall, first to North America, then to Moscow.

He and Stalin spent three weeks discussing how to draw the postwar political map. Churchill suggested the British and the Soviet Union could have "percentages of influence" over different countries: 90 percent for the British in Greece, 90 percent for the Soviets in Romania, 75 percent for the Soviets in Bulgaria, and approximately even splits in Hungary and Yugoslavia. Stalin insisted that Poland would be controlled by the Communists.

From left to right: *The Big Three: Winston Churchill, Franklin D. Roosevelt, and Joseph Stalin. The men met at Yalta to discuss the future of Europe following the war.*

After the German occupiers withdrew from Greece, civil war broke out there between Communist guerrilla fighters and government forces. Churchill (who had just celebrated his seventieth birthday) decided to spend Christmas in Greece, where he helped to resolve the situation.

When the Big Three met again in Yalta, a Russian resort on the Black Sea, in February 1945, Churchill did not feel well and Roosevelt was very frail. The three leaders discussed establishing an organization that became the United Nations and the reparations Germany should pay.

The main discussion centered on the fate of Poland. To Churchill's surprise, Stalin promised that free elections would be held there. After the conference ended, however, it became clear the Soviet leader had lied when Moscow forced a Communist government on

Poland. Churchill became disillusioned, and the alliance between Britain and the Soviet Union dissolved.

Churchill sent a telegram to Roosevelt in mid-March, saying, "Our friendship is the rock on which I build for the peace of the world so long as I am one of the builders." He did not realize the president was too sick to even read it. When Roosevelt died on April 12, Churchill felt a painful and personal loss.

On May 1, the news broke that Hitler, knowing his cause was defeated, had committed suicide. A week later, the Germans surrendered. That afternoon Churchill addressed a huge crowd of cheering Londoners. He told them, "This is your victory. . . . Everyone, man or woman, has done their best."

Thousands of British citizens surround Churchill, center, *to give him thanks for his role in the Allies' victory in Europe in 1945.*

Churchill waves his classic V-sign to a gathering crowd during his run for office in the 1945 general election campaign.

Chapter **SIX**

THE POSTWAR YEARS

WITH THE WAR IN EUROPE AT AN END, CHURCHILL called a general election—the first held in Britain for ten years. His campaign centered on the dangers of Socialism and the Labour Party's policies regarding social programs and state involvement in the economy. But Churchill went too far in a speech broadcast on radio when he charged that a Labour government would bring in a sort of Gestapo to limit free speech and criticism of the government. Since the Gestapo had been the Nazi's secret police force, the comment offended many people.

Britons voted on July 5, but there was a three-week delay to collect and count the votes of members of the scattered armed services before the election results were announced. Meanwhile, Churchill and Labour Party leader Clement Atlee attended a meeting with Stalin and the new U.S. president, Harry Truman, in Potsdam, Germany. When the British politicians returned to London to hear the election results, many people expected Churchill's Conservatives would return to office.

But by noon on the day of the vote count, it was clear that Labour had won in a landslide. No matter how grateful the British people were to Churchill, they wanted a new government to lead the country's postwar recovery. The next morning, Atlee flew back to Potsdam, without Churchill, to continue the conference.

When Clementine suggested the election loss might be a blessing in disguise, Churchill replied, "At the moment, it's certainly very well disguised." Yet he told one assistant, "They are perfectly entitled to vote as they please. This is democracy. This is what we've been fighting for." Still, Churchill missed all the activity of people and reports coming and going. He was disappointed to be out of power with so much still to do to shape the world's postwar future.

On August 6, 1945, a U.S. warplane dropped an atom bomb on Hiroshima, Japan, killing 139,000 people. The U.S. military dropped another atom bomb on Nagasaki three days later. Japan surrendered to the Allies on August 15, and the war was finally over.

In the fall, Clementine began to move their things from the prime minister's residence into the couple's new home in London. Churchill went to Italy and the French Riviera to paint and rest. Over the next few months, however, there was a great deal of tension in the Churchill household.

Churchill was worried about the cost of maintaining Chartwell and again considered selling it. The problem was solved when a group of wealthy friends bought the property and donated it to the National Trust, the organization that owns and preserves historical houses in Great Britain. Churchill could rent the house annually for a small sum for the rest of his life. After his death, it would become a memorial to him.

Churchill remained the leader of the Conservative Party, and his duties in Parliament took some of his time. But much of his energy went into writing *The Second World War*. A team of expert advisers, research assistants, and secretaries helped.

THE "IRON CURTAIN" SPEECH

Churchill and Clementine spent the winter of 1946 in Florida. In March Churchill traveled by train to Fulton, Missouri, at President Truman's invitation, to deliver a lecture at Westminster College. The lecture focused on relations with the Soviet Union.

Churchill warned that "an iron curtain" had descended across the European continent and that the Soviets wanted to expand their power and their policies. He noted that there is nothing the Russians admire so much as strength, and there is nothing for

Prime Minister Churchill delivers his "Iron Curtain" speech in March 1945, in which he warned of the dangers of a Europe divided by Communism.

which they have less respect than weakness. Therefore, he suggested, democracies including the United States, Britain, and members of the British Commonwealth (independent nations and colonies of the diminished British Empire) should cooperate and stand strong together so that no one would attack them.

Many U.S. newspapers reacted negatively to the speech, calling it alarmist. Many people did not want to think about alliances with other nations. But within a short time, the United States changed its attitude toward the Soviet Union, and the so-called Cold War (1945–1991) between Western democracies and Communist countries began.

Churchill gave his next major speech at Zurich University in Switzerland that autumn. His topic was the need for a united Europe and reconciliation between France and Germany.

When the first volume of his war memoirs appeared in 1948, sales on both sides of the Atlantic were strong. Churchill would not have to worry about money anymore. But some of his old insecurities were still there. He told a friend that he wished his father and mother had been alive in 1940 to witness his wartime leadership and see how successful he had become.

In the 1950 general election, the Labour government barely held onto power. Labour prime minister Atlee called another election in 1951. This time, the Conservatives returned to power, and a month before his seventy-seventh birthday, Churchill again became prime minister.

In January 1952, Churchill traveled to Ottawa, Canada, and to Washington, where he met with Truman and addressed the U.S. Congress. He spoke again of the brotherly association between the United States, Britain, and members of the British Commonwealth and of the growing unity in Europe. He also stated that the atom bomb provided the greatest deterrent (means of prevention) to a third world war. It was so powerful and destructive that governments were afraid to engage in war or use it.

Back in Great Britain, Churchill's heart problems returned and he had to reduce his workload. He began thinking of leaving politics. Foreign Minister Anthony Eden, the man everyone expected would succeed him, wanted him to set a date for his resignation.

But Churchill kept finding reasons to stay on. He went to the United States in January 1953 to meet with General Eisenhower, the incoming president, and in June, he attended the coronation of Queen Elizabeth II at Westminster Abbey in London. A few weeks later, a serious stroke partly paralyzed his left side, but the stroke was kept secret. Churchill went to Chartwell, determined to recover, and within a few weeks was able to walk unaided.

The year 1953 brought him many honors. The queen made him a Knight of the Order of the Garter. With this knighthood, he became known as Sir Winston Churchill. Then he learned he was being awarded the Nobel Prize for Literature. Clementine attended the awards ceremony in Stockholm, Sweden, on his behalf, since he was at an important conference in Bermuda.

THE BERMUDA CONFERENCE

The 1953 Bermuda Conference brought together Churchill, U.S. president Dwight Eisenhower, and French prime minister Joseph Laniel to discuss relations with the Soviet Union. Stalin had died that year, so Churchill hoped to relax tensions between the Communists and the United States. Eisenhower believed the Soviets' policy was to destroy capitalists and the free world. The stakes for peace were very high, since the Soviet Union had developed its own atom bomb, and the United States was developing an even more destructive hydrogen bomb. Churchill was unable to convince the U.S. president to talk to the Soviets, and he left the Bermuda Conference disappointed.

Churchill turned eighty in November 1954, and he appeared to be aging rapidly. The pressure to give up the post of prime minister increased from Anthony Eden, from members of Parliament, and from his wife. Finally, on April 5, 1955, Churchill resigned, although he remained a member of Parliament.

He finished writing the four-volume *History of the English-Speaking Peoples.* He spent much of his time visiting with longtime friends, such as Canadian newspaper owner Lord Beaverbrook, in the south of France. Churchill also enjoyed long cruises on the yacht belonging to a new friend, multimillionaire shipowner Aristotle Onassis. He usually brought family members with him, but Clementine did not approve of these friends and their lives of luxury, and the couple was often apart. Churchill's faithful valet brought him his breakfast, ran his bath, helped him dress, and took his dog for walks.

Churchill did not find great happiness in his final years. He became quite deaf and had several more small strokes, a broken hip, and other health problems. He also suffered a recurrence of the depression that had plagued him throughout his life. He believed his life had been a failure. He felt that everything he had done had ended in disaster, his private secretary recalled. Although Churchill had won the war, the British Empire had disappeared, half of Europe was under Communist control, and he worried that Socialism was threatening Great Britain as he knew and loved it.

The lives of several close family members were also troubled. He fought bitterly with Randolph, and except for Mary, his children's marriages ended in divorce. Diana was deeply depressed and committed suicide in 1963. Sarah had alcohol problems. She comforted her father and often sat quietly with him as he seemed to wait for death. "My life is over," he said, "but it is not yet ended."

Nevertheless, Churchill remained a popular figure, especially in the United States. In 1963 Congress voted to make him the first honorary citizen of the United States, and Randolph went to Washington to accept on his father's behalf.

CHURCHILL'S DEATH

On his ninetieth birthday, a frail Churchill struggled to the window to give his famous V sign to the crowd outside his London house, and that evening family members gathered for dinner. On January 10, 1965, he suffered a massive stroke and went into a coma. Silent crowds kept vigil outside the house, and newspapers were filled with the story of his final illness. Two weeks later, on January 24—the seventieth anniversary of his father's death—Churchill died, his wife, children, and grandchildren nearby.

Churchill had begun to plan for his funeral after his 1953 stroke. He chose the hymns that would be sung and requested the military bands that would attend. Over the years, however, the list of people who would

Churchill waves to the press and well-wishers from his home on his ninetieth birthday in November 1964.

carry his coffin had to be altered several times. As one organizer noted, the problem was that Churchill kept living and the pallbearers kept dying.

While his coffin lay in Westminster Hall, two hundred thousand people filed by. Representatives of governments from around the world attended the funeral, and millions watched it on television. Even Queen Elizabeth broke with tradition by attending the funeral of a commoner, a person who wasn't a member of the royalty or nobility. After the service at Saint Paul's Cathedral, the casket was taken across the Thames River by boat, as dockside cranes bowed in respect. A special train then took it to Churchill's final resting place in Bladon churchyard, near Blenheim, next to his father, his mother, and his brother.

CONCLUSION:
MAN OF THE CENTURY

At the end of the twentieth century, many historians, journalists, and other individuals looked back to see which heads rose above the crowd. Winston Churchill's name appeared on almost every list of the most important people of the century.

Most of all, people remember Churchill as the man who, in 1940—after Hitler had overrun Europe—saved Britain and probably democracy. He could not defeat

Churchill gives his V-sign on leaving the office of the prime minister and public life for the last time. He led a distinguished and respected political career.

Hitler without the allies who later joined Britain's side, but he stood firm at that critical time. For many wartime Britons, he was like a symbolic oak tree, with its solid trunk, deep roots, and sheltering arms. Churchill's story continues to inspire people, although he is more popular in the United States than in Britain.

Churchill was never a religious man, but even when his life was in danger as a young soldier, he felt that fate was saving him for some great purpose. Had he resigned when his career was at its depths in 1936 or been killed by that car in New York City, history would have written him off as just another politician who had shown some promise. At the age of sixty-five, he finally found out what that purpose was. And in Adolf Hitler, Churchill had an opponent against whom he could legitimately concentrate all his natural aggressiveness.

Winston Churchill had many great qualities, including energy, perseverance, a sharp memory, enormous powers of concentration, an ability to foresee the future, and great skill as a writer and public speaker. As a government minister, he made a difference in the lives of working people through the social reforms he introduced and in the improved efficiency of the armed forces for which he was responsible. As a statesman, he helped to protect democracy as the world emerged from war and to warn against the threat posed by Communism. As an individual and family man, many people, including his hard-pressed personal staff, loved him dearly.

At a time when the mass media were new, Churchill was an expert media manipulator. As a young man, he sought fame as a means of getting into politics. Later, he used the media, including his own widely read newspaper articles, to deliver his message about the possibility of war. During the war, he spoke on radio and appeared—his fingers in the *V* for victory sign—in newsreels to give people courage.

On the other hand, he has frequently been criticized for lacking good judgment. Some Britons never forgave him for the many soldiers who died in the Dardanelles or for the way he handled the general strike in 1926. During his lifetime, many people, especially members of the Conservative Party, disliked and distrusted him, and he had few close friends. He was often depressed. He was self-centered and never easy to live with or to work for.

This mixture of good and bad qualities make him a fascinating and controversial figure. He was the frequent target of political cartoons in the British press throughout his life and the subject of dozens of biographies later on. But the mixture ultimately made him a strong leader. His self-centeredness meant that, during the 1930s, when all around him ignored the Nazi threat, he had confidence in his own vision.

Despite all that has been written about him, many questions remain. Historians disagree, for example, about whether he was an alcoholic, although there is no question that he consumed alcohol every day. Similarly, some biographers make much of his bouts of deep depression, while others say he was only depressed when circumstances justifiably got him down.

Churchill's life spanned a period of great change. When he was born, Queen Victoria was on the throne of Great Britain and the British Empire stretched around the globe. Neither the telephone nor the motor car nor the electric lightbulb had been invented. When he died, air transportation, television, and antibiotics were commonplace. But Britain was no longer a major economic or political power, and its vast empire was evolving into the British Commonwealth of independent nations. Its World War II allies, the United States and the Soviet Union, were vying to dominate world politics during the Cold War.

Statues of Churchill can be found in public spaces around the world, and streets and parks named in his honor are everywhere. Members of Churchill Societies meet to discuss history and current events, and students have electronic access to massive collections of Churchill's letters, speeches, documents, and articles.

In many parts of the world, people are still fighting for democracy. Nevertheless, the world would be a very different one if Churchill had not been there in 1940 to defy Hitler.

SOURCES

8   Martin Gilbert, *Churchill: A Life* (New York: Henry Holt and Company, 1991), 646.

13   Winston Churchill, *My Early Life, 1874–1904* (New York: Touchstone, 1996), 5.

14   Ibid., 3.

16   Ibid., 15.

17   Ibid., 17.

17   Gilbert, *Churchill: A Life*, 20.

18   Ibid., 38.

18   Ibid., 40.

20   Churchill, *My Early Life*, 62.

27   Ibid., 252.

31   Gilbert, *Churchill: A Life*, 146.

31   Roy Jenkins, *Churchill. A Biography* (New York: Plume, 2001), 137.

32   William Manchester, *The Last Lion: Winston Spencer Churchill; Alone: 1932–1940* (New York: Delta, 1988), 104–105.

39   Gilbert, *Churchill: A Life*, 268.

43   Ibid., 321.

44   Ibid., 323.

44   Manchester, *The Last Lion*, 22.

46   Ibid., 411.

47   Ibid., 438.

49   Ibid., 454.

64   Ibid., 196.

68   Gilbert, *Churchill: A Life*, 608.

69   Ibid., 620.

55   Manchester, *The Last Lion*, 17.

71   Gilbert, *Churchill: A Life*, 627.

72   Ibid., 645.

73   Ibid., 656.

76   Ibid., 664.

77   Ibid., 671.

78   Ibid., 665.

80 John Keegan, *Winston Churchill: A Penguin Life* (Harmondsworth, UK: Lipper/Viking, 2002), 43.

80 Gilbert, *Churchill: A Life*, 702.

82 Ibid., 718.

83 Ibid., 727.

84 Ibid., 734.

86 Keegan, *Winston Churchill*, 170.

89 Gilbert, *Churchill: A Life*, 831.

89 "The War Time Speeches of Winston Churchill," *The Churchill Society*, London, n.d., http://www.churchill-society-london.org.uk/NEVER.html, (July 11, 2005).

92 Jenkins, *Churchill. A Biography*, 798.

92 Gilbert, *Churchill: A Life*, 856.

98 Ibid., 956.

SELECTED BIBLIOGRAPHY

Churchill, Winston. *My Early Life, 1874–1904*. Introduction by William Manchester. New York: Touchstone, 1996.

Gilbert, Martin. *Churchill: A Life*. New York: Henry Holt and Company, 1991.

Jenkins, Roy. *Churchill: A Biography*. New York: Plume, 2001.

Keegan, John. *Winston Churchill: A Penguin Life*. Harmondsworth, UK: Lipper/Viking, 2002.

Lukacs, John. *Churchill: Visionary, Statesman, Historian*. New Haven, CT: Yale University Press, 2002.

Manchester, William. *The Last Lion: Winston Spencer Churchill; Alone: 1932–1940*. New York: Delta, 1988.

Ramsden, John. *Man of the Century: Winston Churchill and His Legend Since 1945*. London: HarperCollins, 2002.

Rubin, Gretchen. *Forty Ways to Look at Winston Churchill. A Brief Account of a Long Life*. New York: Ballantine Books, 2003.

FURTHER READING
AND WEBSITES

BOOKS

Altman, Linda Jacobs. *Adolf Hitler: Evil Mastermind of the Holocaust*. Berkeley Heights, NJ: Enslow, 2005.

Churchill, Sarah. *A Thread in the Tapestry*. London: Andre Deutsch, 1967.

Churchill, Winston S. *The Second World War. Illustrated & Abridged*. Kent, UK: Grange Books, 2003.

Dutton, David. *Neville Chamberlain*. New York: Oxford University Press, 2001.

Goldstein, Margaret J. *World War II—Europe*. Minneapolis: Lerner Publications Company, 2004.

Humes, James C. *Biography. Winston Churchill*. New York: DK Publishing, 2003.

Pearson, John. *The Private Lives of Winston Churchill*. Toronto: Viking, 1991.

Roberts, Jeremy. *Franklin D. Roosevelt*. Minneapolis: Lerner Publications Company, 2002.

Zuehlke, Jeffrey. *Joseph Stalin*. Minneapolis: Twenty-First Century Books, 2006.

WEBSITES

The Churchill Center
  http://www.churchill.org
  The Washington-based Churchill Center's website features classroom activities focusing on leadership qualities, the myths that have grown up around Churchill, and the relevance of Churchill to the United States. The site also has links to recent news stories and articles about Churchill.

The Churchill Society, London
  http://www.churchill-society-london.org.uk/1940MJJA.html
  This huge, well-illustrated website includes a description of
  Churchill's life, audio and text excerpts from his speeches,
  chronologies of the two world wars, and reference materials
  designed specifically for schools.
Churchill: The Evidence
  http://www.nls.uk/digital library/churchill
  This online exhibit features interesting documents from the
  life and times of Winston Churchill. It was prepared by the
  National Library of Scotland, the Churchill Archives Centre,
  home to a vast collection of letters and papers stored at the
  University of Cambridge.
Sir Winston Churchill (1874–1965)
  http://www.bbc.co.uk/history/historic_figures/churchill_winston
  .shtml
  This BBC website has links to articles and multimedia
  features relating to Churchill's era, the war, and other historic
  figures.

INDEX

OTHER TITLES FROM LERNER AND A&E®:

Ariel Sharon
Arnold Schwarzenegger
Arthur Ashe
The Beatles
Benito Mussolini
Benjamin Franklin
Bill Gates
Bruce Lee
Carl Sagan
Chief Crazy Horse
Christopher Reeve
Colin Powell
Daring Pirate Women
Edgar Allan Poe
Eleanor Roosevelt
Fidel Castro
Frank Gehry
George Lucas
George W. Bush
Gloria Estefan
Hillary Rodham Clinton
Jack London
Jacques Cousteau
Jane Austen
Jesse Owens
Jesse Ventura
Jimi Hendrix
J. K. Rowling
John Glenn
Joseph Stalin
Latin Sensations

Legends of Dracula
Legends of Santa Claus
Louisa May Alcott
Madeleine Albright
Malcolm X
Mao Zedung
Mark Twain
Maya Angelou
Mohandas Gandhi
Mother Teresa
Napoleon Bonaparte
Nelson Mandela
Oprah Winfrey
Osama bin Laden
Pope John Paul II
Princess Diana
Queen Cleopatra
Queen Elizabeth I
Queen Latifah
Rosie O'Donnell
Saddam Hussein
Saint Joan of Arc
Thurgood Marshall
Tiger Woods
Tony Blair
Vladimir Putin
William Shakespeare
Wilma Rudolph
Women in Space
Women of the Wild West
Yasser Arafat

ABOUT THE AUTHOR

Janice Hamilton began her writing career as a newspaper journalist. She has written ten nonfiction books for young readers, focusing on history and geography. Hamilton lives in Montreal, Canada.

PHOTO ACKNOWLEDGMENTS

The images in this book are used with the permission of: © Fox Photos/Hulton Archive, Getty Images, p. 2; The Illustrated London News, pp. 6, 89; © H.F. Davis/Topical Press Agency/Hulton Archive, Getty Images, p. 8; © Hulton Archive, Getty Images, pp. 10, 34, 36, 42, 50; Library of Congress, pp. 13 (LC-DIG-ppmsca-04654), 17 (LC-DIG-ppmsca-04654), 28 (LC-US62-65632), 30 (LC-USZ62-75523), 33 (LC-USZ62-75526), 73 (LC-USZ62-132602), 79 (LC-USE6-D-001276); © Bettmann/CORBIS, pp. 15, 20, 40, 87; © Hulton-Deutsch Collection/CORBIS, pp. 22, 25, 38, 100; © Topical Press Agency/ Hulton Archives, Getty Images, pp. 48, 52, 57; United States Holocaust Memorial Museum (USHMM), pp. 60 (courtesy of Estelle Bechoefer), 68 (courtesy of Richard A. Rupert); National Archives, pp. 63, 81 (W&C 1047), 88 (NWDNS-111-SC-260486); © CORBIS, p. 67; © G.R. Greated/Fox Photos/Hulton Archive, Getty Images, p. 70; © Topham/The Image Works, p. 74; © Keystone/Hulton Archive, Getty Images, pp. 75, 99; © Underwood & Underwood/ CORBIS, p. 90; AP/WideWorld Photos, p. 94.

Cover: Library of Congress (LC-USW33-019093-C). Back cover: Library of Congress (LC-DIG.ggbain-04739).

WEBSITES

Website addresses in this book were valid at the time of printing. However, because of the nature of the Internet, some addresses may have changed or sites may have closed since publication. While the author and Publisher regret any inconvenience this may cause readers, no responsibility for any such changes can be accepted by the author or Publisher.